DEAD-
POOL
WHAT HAPPENED
IN VEGAS

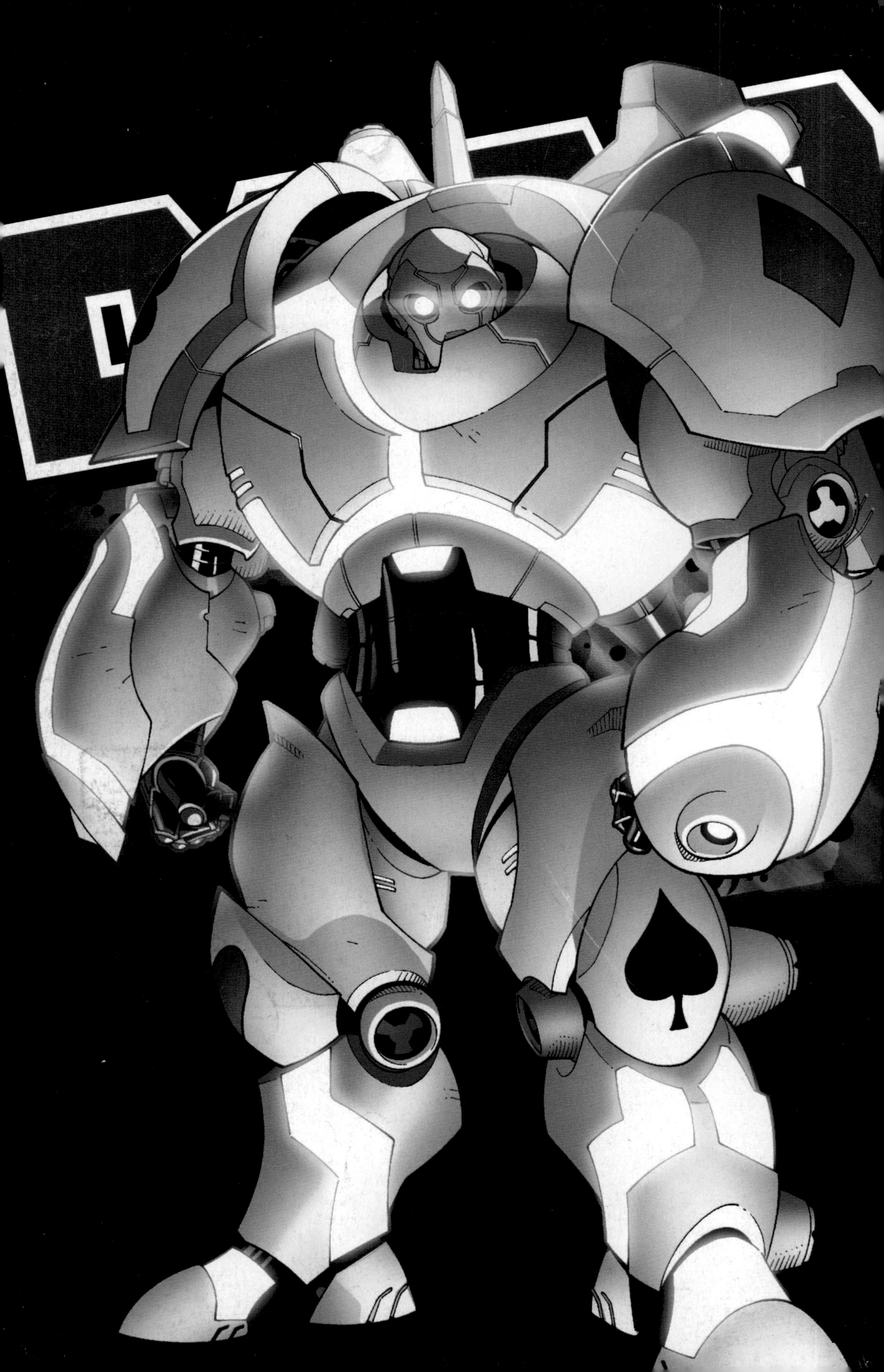

DOL

WHAT HAPPENED IN VEGAS

WRITER: **DANIEL WAY** • PENCILS: **CARLO BARBERI**
INKS: **JUAN VLASCO** • COLORS: **MARTE GRACIA**
LETTERS: **VIRTUAL CALLIGRAPHY'S JOE SABINO**
COVER ARTISTS: **JASON PEARSON** & **DAVE JOHNSON**

"WADE UNTIL DARK"

WRITER: **DUANE SWIERCZYNSKI** • ART: **PHILIP BOND**
COLORS: **LEE LOUGHRIDGE**
LETTERS: **VIRTUAL CALLIGRAPHY'S JOE SABINO**

ASSISTANT EDITOR: **JODY LEHEUP**
EDITOR: **AXEL ALONSO**

DEADPOOL CREATED BY ROB LIEFELD AND FABIAN NICIEZA

COLLECTION EDITOR: **CORY LEVINE**
ASSISTANT EDITORS: **ALEX STARBUCK** & **NELSON RIBEIRO**
EDITORS, SPECIAL PROJECTS: **JENNIFER GRÜNWALD** & **MARK D. BEAZLEY**
SENIOR EDITOR, SPECIAL PROJECTS: **JEFF YOUNGQUIST**
SVP OF PRINT & DIGITAL PUBLISHING SALES: **DAVID GABRIEL**
BOOK DESIGN: **RODOLFO MURAGUCHI**

EDITOR IN CHIEF: **AXEL ALONSO**
CHIEF CREATIVE OFFICER: **JOE QUESADA**
PUBLISHER: **DAN BUCKLEY**
EXECUTIVE PRODUCER: **ALAN FINE**

EADPOOL VOL. 5: WHAT HAPPENED IN VEGAS. Contains material originally published in magazine form as DEADPOOL #23-26. Third printing 2014. ISBN# 978-0-7851-4533-2. Published by MARVEL WORLDWIDE, C., a subsidiary of MARVEL ENTERTAINMENT, LLC. OFFICE OF PUBLICATION: 135 West 50th Street, New York, NY 10020. **Printed in the U.S.A.** ALAN FINE, EVP - Office of the President, Marvel Worldwide, c. and EVP & CMO Marvel Characters B.V.; DAN BUCKLEY, Publisher & President - Print, Animation & Digital Divisions; JOE QUESADA, Chief Creative Officer; TOM BREVOORT, SVP of Publishing; DAVID BOGART, SVP of perations & Procurement, Publishing; C.B. CEBULSKI, SVP of Creator & Content Development; DAVID GABRIEL, SVP of Print & Digital Publishing Sales; JIM O'KEEFE, VP of Operations & Logistics; DAN CARR, Executive rector of Publishing Technology; SUSAN CRESPI, Editorial Operations Manager; ALEX MORALES, Publishing Operations Manager; STAN LEE, Chairman Emeritus. For information regarding advertising in Marvel Comics on Marvel.com, please contact Niza Disla, Director of Marvel Partnerships, at ndisla@marvel.com. For Marvel subscription inquiries, please call 800-217-9158. **Manufactured between 11/6/2013 and 12/9/2013 R.R. DONNELLEY, INC., SALEM, VA, USA.**

9 8 7 6 5 4 3

23

DEADPOOL #23 HEROIC AGE VARIANT
by Chris Giarrusso

--LIVE FROM THE POPPY FIELD NIGHTCLUB IN LAS VEGAS AS TONIGHT, PEOPLE OF THE WORLD ARE UNITED IN JOYOUS CELEBRATION UPON LEARNING OF THE REUNIFICATION OF EARTH'S MIGHTIEST HEROES, THE ORIGINAL AVENGERS!
TRULY, THIS IS THE DAWN OF A NEW AND, FINALLY, HEROIC AGE.
YEAH, MAN... ALL THIS GRIM AN' GRITTY STUFF? ALL THESE SUPPOSEDLY "GOOD GUYS" WHO DO BAD THINGS IN ORDER TO DO GOOD? THAT'S OVER, MAN!
IT'S TIME TO LEEEEET THE LIGHT SHIIIINE! LEEEEET THE LIGHT SHINE IIINN!
PUNISHER? YEAH, RIGHT... THAT GUY IS SCARY AND GROSS. GIVE ME THOR ANY DAY!
WOOT! WOOT! HOLLAH ATCHA GIRL!
IT'S JUST...IT'S JUST THE WAY IT OUGHTTA BE, RIGHT? I MEAN, WE'VE BEEN WITHOUT OUR HEROES FOR TOO LONG, MAN! WHO'RE THE KIDS SUPPOSED TO BE LOOKIN' UP TO, HUH?
LONZO TOUTOLOS – CLUB OWNER
'CAUSE IT SURE AIN'T DIRTBAGS LIKE DEADPOOL...

NEXT DAY.
POPPY FIELD. THAT'S RIGHT.
NO, I DON'T NEED THE NUMBER...
WELCOME TO Fabulous LAS VEGAS NEVADA
LV MCHN
...JUST AN ADDRESS.
TRICKY
RT ONE: HERE COMES A NEW SHOOTER

You know we can't bring guns in there...
NOT GONNA NEED ANY GUNS-- JUST GONNA SMACK THE GUY AROUND FOR DEFAMING ME, IS ALL.
WHAT'S THE POINT OF THAT?
I DUNNO.
LVMCHN
WHAT'S THE POINT OF THAT?
I'LL GIVE YOU FIVE GRAND FOR THE OXYGEN TANK.
UHH...
AND THREE GRAND FOR THE SUNGLASSES.

HI, THERE.
YOU KNOW WHO I AM?
T ME THINK...ARE
OU THE GUY WHO
BROKE INTO MY
OFFICE?
YES.
ARE YOU THE GUY WHO DOESN'T KNOW THAT THE COSTUME PARTY WAS LAST NIGHT?
OH, I KNOW ALL ABOUT THE COSTUME PARTY LAST NIGHT--I SAW IT ON TV.
MY TURN.
ARE YOU THE GUY THAT DEFAMED ME? CALLED ME A..."DIRTBAG," I BELIEVE IT WAS?
ARE YOU... ARE YOU REALLY DEADPOOL?
C'MON, LONZO... THAT'S NOT WHAT YOU REALLY WANNA ASK. GO AHEAD AN' SPIT IT OUT.
ARE... YOU GONNA KILL ME?
THAT'S MORE LIKE IT...

SEE YOU HAVE A PANIC BUTTON HERE...YOU PUSH THIS AND IT SENDS A SIGNAL TO CASINO SECURITY, RIGHT?
I'M THINKING YOU'D REEEALLY LIKE TO PUSH IT RIGHT ABOUT NOW...AM I RIGHT?
Y-YEAH.
WELL?
GO AHEAD.
BUT I WARN YOU...
...BAD THINGS WILL HAPPEN.
LOOK, MAN... I'M SORRY FOR WHAT I SAID, OKAY?
I...I DON'T WANT ANY TROUBLE.
OH, YOU DON'T?
WELL, THEN I GUESS I SHOULD LEAVE.

H-HEH.
GOOD LUCK GETTIN' OUT THE DOOR, #@@HOLE...
CHK
BOOOOM!
What next?
GAMBLING OR ALL-YOU-CAN-EAT BUFFET?
ARE WE PACKING ANYTHING TO COMBAT EXPLOSIVE DIARRHEA?
Nope.
THEN THEY'RE BOTH A GAMBLE. LET'S GO WITH OPTION "A."

MINUTES LATER.
SECURITY
WHAT THE HELL JUST HAPPENED?! GET THAT IDIOT CLUB OWNER DOWN HERE--I WANT ANSWERS!
SIR, THE FIRE DEPARTMENT IS HERE...
TELL 'EM TO WAIT! TELL 'EM IT WAS A MINOR GAS LEAK, BUT WE HAVE IT UNDER CONTROL!
THEY'RE STILL GONNA WANT TO--
THEN STALL 'EM!
I DON'T WANT ANYBODY IN THERE UNTIL I KNOW WHAT THEY'RE GONNA FIND. I HAVE MILLIONS OF DOLLARS IN PLAY OUT ON THE GAMING FLOOR...IF THEY SHUT ME DOWN...
WE HAVE... ANOTHER PROBLEM, SIR.
OH, GOD--WHAT NOW?!
THIS GUY OUT ON THE FLOOR...HE'S BETTING LIKE A LUNATIC.
SO? GOOD!
BUT HE'S WINNING.
"A LOT."
I LOVE THIS GAME!
What's not to love?
IT'S GOT RED, IT'S GOT BLACK, IT'S WILDLY UNPREDICTABLE...
"THAT'S NOT ANOTHER PROBLEM--IT'S THE SAME PROBLEM.
"THAT'S DEADPOOL."

THE MERCENARY? THE GUY WHO--?
CAN YOU HANDLE HIM?
YEP.
AND THERE'S NO WAY IT'S A COINCIDENCE THAT HE'S HERE AT THE SAME TIME SOMETHING'S EXPLODING.
IT'D BE MY PLEASURE.

OKAY, BUT NOT IN MY CASINO, UNDERSTAND?
OF COURSE NOT. I'LL LURE HIM OUTSIDE.
HOW?
"GONNA NEED SOME HELP ON THAT ONE..."
...AND IN JUST A FEW MOMENTS, CONTESTANTS FROM THE INAUGURAL BEA ARTHUR LOOK-ALIKE CONTEST WILL BE APPEARING JUST OUTSIDE THE MAIN LOBBY DOORS!
EXIT
VENUS
CLEAR THE LANE!
COMIN' THROUGH!
OH, YOU GOTTA BE KIDDING ME...
HE DOESN'T LOOK ANYTHING LIKE BEA ARTHUR!

--ABOVE THE STRIP AS WE SEE THE MERCENARY DEADPOOL GOING TOE-TO-TOE WITH SIN CITY'S NEWEST HERO-IN-RESIDENCE...
"...THE HOUSE!"
"THE HOUSE?!"
THAT'S THE BEST YOU COULD DO?!
I CAN DO A LOT BETTER THAN THAT, WADE...
WELCOME TO LAS VEGAS.
WHERE THE HOUSE ALWAYS WINS.

HE CALLED US "WADE."
This guy knows us.
AND THAT MEANS...
I... KNOW YOU...
YOU KNEW THE OLD ME.
DOES THE OLD YOU...HAVE A NAME?
VVVVMMMMM--
YEAH.
WEASEL.
GUESS WHAT, "OLD BUDDY"?
I'M A HERO NOW.

43 MINUTES LATER...
UNNHH...
WHERE...?
SSSHINK!
AAOOOOWW!
WHAT THE HELL WAS TH--
SHUKK!
OUCH! DAMMIT!
OH, I GET IT...
...YOU MADE A BOX?
YUP.
Do you think readers will remember what "the box" is? That it's a torture device with no light inside, filled with razor-sharp objects that make movement almost impossible?
JUST FOR ME?
IF THEY DO, THEY'LL ALSO REMEMBER THAT WE LOCKED WEASEL IN ONE A FEW YEARS AGO AND...KINDA LEFT HIM THERE.
YUP.
I'VE BEEN KEEPING IT IN STORAGE.

I THOUGHT YOU WERE OVER ALL OF THAT...
OH, I'M OVER IT--BELIEVE ME. BUT IT'S A GOOD THING I KEPT IT BECAUSE...WELL, I COULDN'T EXACTLY TAKE YOU TO JAIL, NOW COULD I?
GOOD POINT.
BUT Y'KNOW WHAT YOU COULD DO...
WHAT'S THAT?
GO #$%* YOURSELF.
Y'MEAN, LIKE YOU DID?
YOU SHOULDN'T HAVE COME TO VEGAS, WADE...THIS IS MY CITY, NOW. I'M ITS PROTECTOR-- ITS HERO.
I WOULD CLAP FOR YOU, BUT...Y'KNOW...
OUTTA CURIOSITY, WHAT'S A GIG LIKE THAT PAY?
PFFT!
YOU WOULDN'T BELIEVE ME IF I TOLD YOU.
TRY ME.

HOW'D YOU--?!
YOU WOULDN'T BELIEVE ME IF I TOLD YOU.
GOT A *PROPOSITION* FOR YA, WEASEL.
THINK YOU'RE GONNA LIKE IT.
...AND IF I DON'T?
HMMM... LEMME THINK ABOUT THAT...
OKAY, IF YOU SAY "*NO*"?
I'M GONNA GO TO WORK ON YOU WITH THAT BIG HAMMER OVER THERE.

BUT IF YOU SAY "YES"?
YOU'LL BE MAKIN' TWICE AS MUCH AS YOU ARE NOW.
BUT... HOW?
EASY, WEASE-Y.
EXPANSION.
YOU GOT TWO OF THESE THINGS... MIGHT AS WELL USE 'EM, RIGHT?
Y'MEAN... YOU?
I MEAN US.
PARTNER.

"OKAY...DEAL--BUT FIRST, LEMME TELL YOU A FEW THINGS ABOUT THIS CITY, AND WHAT IT IS I DO."
--BUSTED OUT TWO DAYS AGO. GOIN' TO PICK UP SOME SCRATCH, GET BACK ON MY FEET.
"WHEN SUPER VILLAINS NEED MONEY, THEY DON'T GO TO THE BANK.
"THEY COME HERE."
YEAH. GONNA KNOCK OVER A CASINO.
LITERALLY.
WOW, THAT IS A GOOD IDEA! WISH I'D THOUGHT OF DOIN' THAT...
WELL, I DID--WHATTA YOU THINK BROUGHT ME HERE?

"BUT ONCE I GOT HERE, A BETTER IDEA OCCURRED TO ME--WHY TAKE DOWN ONE CASINO...
BOOOOOMMMMMM!
"...WHEN I CAN GET A PIECE OF ALL OF 'EM?"
LOOKS LIKE YOU WENT AFTER THE WRONG PIC-A-NIC BASKET, GRIZZLY.
IT'S THE HOUSE!
THAT GUY'S #$&#$%' AWESOME!
"A PROTECTION RACKET?"
"NO, A PROTECTION SERVICE, SPONSORED BY THE CASINOS. ALL I WANTED WAS THE MONEY...
"...I NEVER EXPECTED TO BE REGARDED AS A HERO."

TWO HUNDRED ON THE HOUSE TO WIN-- ANY TAKERS?
HELL, NO...
KROKK!
UHH... ON SECOND THOUGHT...
LOOK, NEW KID--I AIN'T SOME CHUMP. I'VE BEEN AROUND.
I'VE FOUGHT 'EM ALL, AN' I'M STILL STANDIN'.
G-AAAHH!
QUOTE ELTON JOHN AGAIN, AN' IT'LL BE EVEN WORSE.

WHO'S THAT?
LADIES AND GENTLEMEN, I'D LIKE TO INTRODUCE...
...WILDCARD!
MY NEW SIDEKICK.

WE NEVER DISCUSSED "SIDEKICK."
WE DIDN'T?
NO.
WE DISCUSSED "HAMMER."
GULP!
THOUGHT YA COULD OUBLE-TEAM ME, HUH? OUPLA GRANDSTANDIN' JERKS...
...LEMME SHOW YA HOW THE GRIZZ HANDLES HIS BUSINESS.
OH, MY GOD, HE'S GOING TO...

...HUG HIM?!
HE'S CRUSHING THE SUIT! ACTIVATE THE REPULSOR FIELD, WADE!
WHICH BUTTON IS THAT?!
K-KRAK!
LEFT INDEX FINGER!
PINNG!
WHAT THE--?
WWRRROOOSSCHH!
DAMMIT, WADE-- THAT'S YOUR RIGHT INDEX FINGER!
HEH-HEH...
JUST YOU AN' ME NOW, TIN MAN...
YEP... IMAGINE THAT.
VVVVMMMMM
SO, HOW'VE YA BEEN?

DEAD-POOL?!
GOT A PROPOSITION FOR YA, GRIZZ.
THINK YOU'RE GONNA LIKE IT.

24
Fabulous
AS VEGAS
NEVAD

--SIN CITY'S NEWEST HERO, WILDCARD, WHO QUICKLY TOOK CONTROL OF THE SITUATION, TAKING THE WOULD-BE ROBBER OUTSIDE...
...FOR A MUCH-DESERVED NEVADA BUTT-WHUPPIN'.
WILL THIS RIDICULOUS BEAR-MAN BE BACK? WE DON'T KNOW. BUT WITH WILDCARD NOW HERE TO PROTECT US...
KLIK!
GOTTA SAY, WEASEL, WE HAD OUR DOUBTS ABOUT THIS NEW PARTNER OF YOURS BUT... WHAT CAN I SAY?
HE'S A HIT.
AND FRANKLY, HE CAME OUT LOOKING A HELLUVA LOT BETTER THAN YOU DID...

WHO ARE YOU, ANYWAY?
YOU CAN TELL US, DON'T WORRY-- WE'LL KEEP YOUR IDENTITY A SECRET, JUST LIKE WE DO FOR WEASEL.
UH, I THINK WILDCARD WOULD RATHER REMAIN ANONYMOUS, EVEN FROM Y--
VZZT--!
HI.
MY NAME'S DEADPOOL. PERHAPS YOU'VE HEARD OF ME...?
TRICKY
PART TWO: THE BIG BLIND

WHAT'RE YOU DOING?! WE AGREED THAT YOU WOULDN'T--!
HEY, WHAT'S THE BIG DEAL?
THE BIG DEAL...
...IS THAT YOU'RE--GULP!--DEADPOOL.
SO?
YOU'RE... A MANIAC. AND...
...EVERYONE HATES YOU.
DO YOU HONESTLY THINK WE'RE GOING TO ALLOW YOU TO ROAM OUR CASINOS IN A SUPER-POWERED ARMORED SUIT?
DO YOU HONESTLY THINK YOU HAVE A CHOICE?
YOU HAVE A POINT.
WE'LL CONTINUE TO HONOR OUR AGREEMENTS, PROVIDED YOU CONTINUE TO HONOR YOURS.
NOW, IF YOU WOULD EXCUSE US, MR. DEADPOOL... WE'D LIKE TO TALK TO WEASEL.
ALONE.
COOL!
SEE YA BACK AT HQ, BUDDY!

BACK AT HQ:
THANKS A LOT, YOU #$%& JERK!
WHOA! LANGUAGE!
FIRST, YOU MAKE ME LOOK LIKE A DUMBASS ON TV, AND THEN I GET MY BUTT CHEWED FOR HALF AN HOUR BECAUSE OF YOU!
BUT YOU DON'T CARE ABOUT THAT, DO YOU? MUST BE NICE, BEIN' THE ONE WHO GETS ALL THE GLORY!
HELL-YEAH IT IS! LOOK AT THE PRESS I'M GETTIN', DUDE--THEY LOVE ME!
I'M NEW! I'M HOT! I'M FRESH OUT THE BOX!
I CAN DO NO WRONG!
WADE, I KNOW YOU--EVERYTHING YOU DO IS WRONG.
OKAY, OKAY, OKAY...MAYBE I DID KINDA SHOW YOU UP BIG-TIME. I'M SORRY.
AN' LOOK, I DON'T WANT ANY HARD FEELINGS, SO...HOW ABOUT THIS?
WE SWITCH.

WE SWITCH SUITS! YOU'LL BE WILDCARD AN' I'LL BE THE HOUSE! WHO'S GONNA KNOW THE DIFFERENCE?
HUH?
UH, THE CASINO OWNERS?
NOT IF WE DON'T TELL 'EM...
SO...I'M GONNA BE THE SIDEKICK?
EMBRACE YOUR DESTINY, MY FRIEND.
EMBRACE IT.
HRRONNNK! HRRONNNK! HRRONNK!
WHAT THE HELL IS THAT?!
THERE'S A SITUATION!

LET'S SEE...
TEK! TEK! TIK!
...WELL, WHATTA YA KNOW.
HE'S BACK.
THEN WHAT'RE YA WAITIN' FOR?
LET'S GO SPANK HIS BEAR-ASS.

WHAT, YA THOUGHT YA COULD JUST SHOW UP AN' SPANK MY ASS?
KRRUNCHH!
THINK AGAIN.
THIS TIME, I KNEW YOU WAS COMIN'.
GAAHH--!
GHOOMM

YOU BACK-SHOOTIN' SON OF A--
AH-AH-AH...
WATCH YOUR MOUTH.
KROOKK!
DUDE, GET UP! YOU'RE MAKIN' ME LOOK BAD!
DON'T WORRY ABOUT ME--!
I'M NOT! I'M WORRIED ABOUT ME... THE OL' SWITCHEROO, REMEMBER? I CAN'T HAVE PEOPLE THINKIN' THAT--
DAMMIT, HE'S GETTING AWAY!
RUNNING AWAY IS MORE LIKE IT...
HE'S HEADED FOR THE COUNTING ROOM!
C'MON!
THE WHAAA--?!
THE COUNTING ROOM, YOU IDIOT!

"IT'S WHERE THEY KEEP ALL THE CASH!"
BAG IT UP, #%$*-HEADS.

HEH-HEH-HEH... JACKPOT.
SAVOR THE MOMENT, BEAR BOY, BECAUSE THE ONLY WAY YOU'RE GONNA MAKE IT OUTTA THERE...
...IS THROUGH US.
WHY DID YOU JUST TELL HIM THAT...?
BWHOOOOOOMMMMM

UNNNHH...
C'MON! HE'S MAKIN' OFF WITH THE LOOT!
NOT TONIGHT...HAVE A HEADACHE...
JACKPOT
YOU'RE GIVING UP?!
YOU SHOULD BE ASHAMED OF YOURSELF.
Y'know what?
WE KINDA ARE.
OUTTA THE WAY, SUCKERS!
WHY DO THEY MAKE IT SO HARD TO GET OUTTA THESE FRICKIN' PLACES?!
LEMME HELP YOU WITH THAT...

KA-RR-ROOMMM!
IT'S WILDCARD!
ENTRACE
"BUT WHERE'S THE HOUSE?"
DRINKS...
NEED DRINKS OVER HERE...

WHAT THE HELL IS WEASEL DOING?!
NOTHING, FROM WHAT I CAN TELL...
...OH, WAIT.
HE'S DRINKING A LIME RICKEY.
THAT LITTLE SCUMBAG--!
WELL, AT LEAST WE'VE GOT WILDCARD...
SURE, HE'S CAUSED A BIT MORE STRUCTURAL DAMAGE THAN WE WOULD'VE LIKED, BUT AT LEAST HE'S HOLDING HIS OWN AGAINST...
...WHAT'S HIS NAME?
"GRIZZLY."
OKAY.

W-WAIT...
WAIT FOR WHAT?
FOR MY REPULSOR RAY TO CHARGE, SUCKER--!
BLASH!
HEH-HEH... THAT ALL YA BROUGHT TO THE PARTY?

KLAK
KLAK
KLAK
KLAK
KLIK!
NOPE.

I AM SO SICK OF PEOPLE LIKE YOU.
YOU PREY ON PEOPLE'S GOOD NATURE. THEIR TRUST.
YOU TAKE EVERYTHING YOU CAN AND YOU DON'T GIVE ANYTHING BACK.
YOU'RE JUST LIKE HIM.
YOU'RE A BULLY.
HOW'S IT FEEL TO BE ON THE OTHER END OF IT FOR ONCE?
OH, #&$%...
HE'S GONNA %&$# WASTE HIM...

THIS IS GONNA BE BAD...
A P.R. NIGHTMARE...
LVPD IS NOT GONNA LIKE THIS...
THERE'S GONNA BE INVESTIGATIONS...
FEDERAL...
I KNEW WE COULDN'T TRUST DEADPOOL...
OH, GOD.
"HERE IT COMES..."
HOONNNK!
YYYAAAAAAAYYYYYY!

YEAH!
YEEEAAHH!
LET'S HEAR IT FOR ME AND MY BOY!
WOOT! WOOT!
ve Night
ve Night
BOOOOO!
SO IT'S LIKE THAT?
AFTER ALL I'VE DONE FOR YOU? AFTER ALL THE TIMES I'VE SAVED THIS CRAPPY, CARD-CHEATIN' LITTLE TOWN OF YOURS?
YOU'RE GONNA TURN ON ME?!
I SAVED YOUR WHOLE #%&$ PLANET!

DUDE.
NO, YOU DIDN'T...
CHILL.
THERE ARE CAMERAS HERE, OKAY? THIS IS NOT THE TIME TO FREAK OUT.
OH, I DISAGREE, PARTNER...
CHOOOOOOMMMM!
KRRUNNNCHH
THIS IS THE PERFECT TIME TO FREAK OUT.

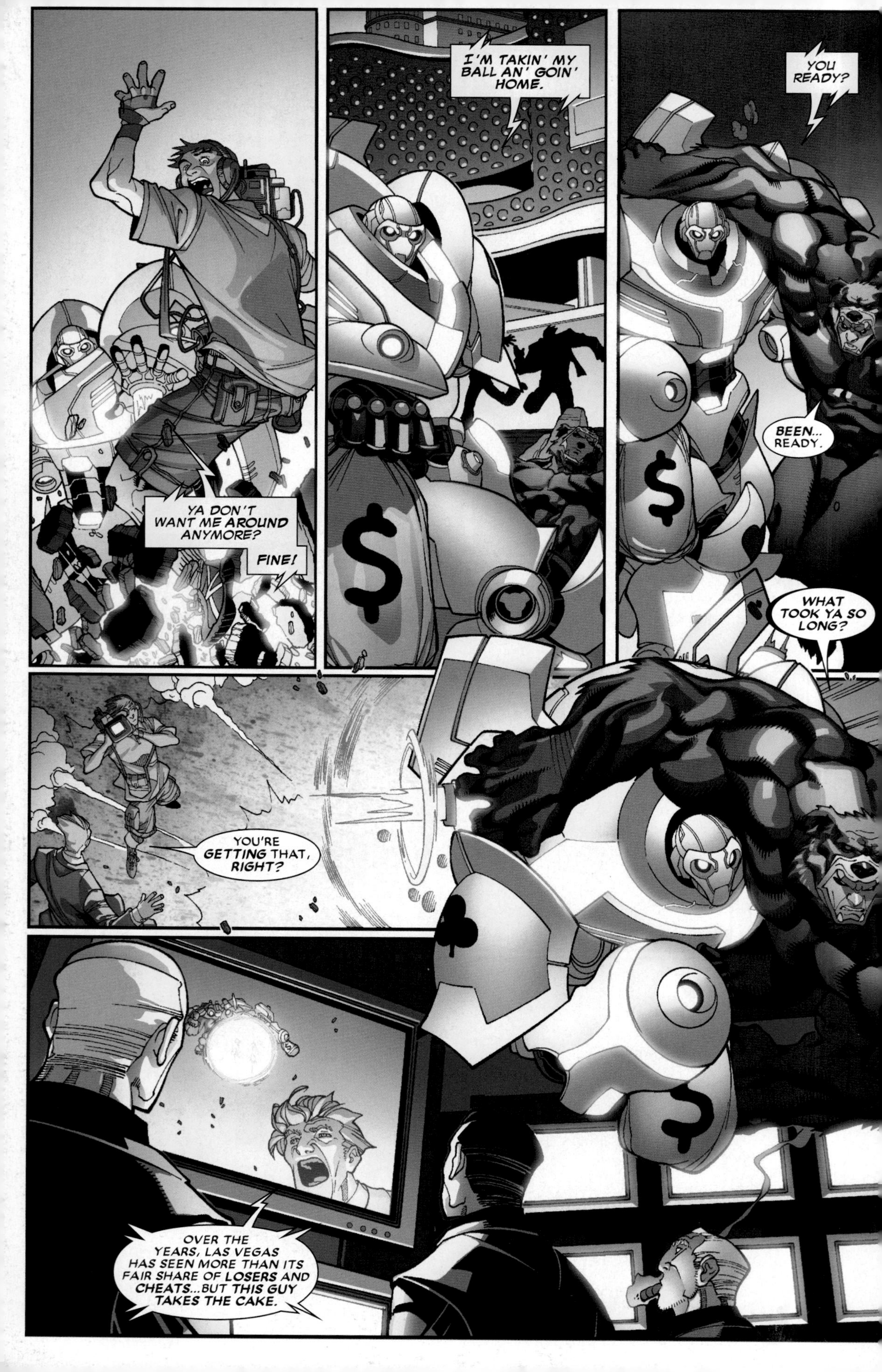
YA DON'T WANT ME AROUND ANYMORE?
FINE!
I'M TAKIN' MY BALL AN' GOIN' HOME.
YOU READY?
BEEN... READY.
WHAT TOOK YA SO LONG?
YOU'RE GETTING THAT, RIGHT?
OVER THE YEARS, LAS VEGAS HAS SEEN MORE THAN ITS FAIR SHARE OF LOSERS AND CHEATS...BUT THIS GUY TAKES THE CAKE.

JACK HAMMER...A.K.A., WEASEL.
HOW APPROPRIATE.
BREAKING NEWS
CNV
LAS VEGAS BIGGEST CHEATER
BARBERI FIRST LIVE CRASH DUMMY TO GO TO MARS
WE'VE RECEIVED CONFIRMATION THAT MR. HAMMER IS, IN FACT, THE SECRET IDENTITY OF THE NOW FORMER SUPER HERO, THE HOUSE, WHO TODAY WAS CAPTURED ON VIDEO CONSPIRING WITH THE SUPER-CRIMINAL GRIZZLY TO STEAL AN UNDISCLOSED--BUT ASSUMEDLY LARGE--SUM OF CASH FROM ONE OF THE LOCAL CASINOS.
HAMMER'S WHEREABOUTS ARE CURRENTLY UNKNOWN, BUT STATE AND LOCAL INVESTIGATORS ARE WORKING WITH THE CASINO OWNERS FOR WHOM HAMMER HAD PREVIOUSLY BEEN WORKING...
...PRIOR TO HIS GRIEVOUS BETRAYAL OF BOTH THEIR TRUST, AND THE TRUST OF THE PEOPLE OF LAS VEGAS.
WOW.
DO YOU KNOW WHERE HE IS?
NOPE. HAVEN'T SEEN HIM SINCE I...SINCE HE PUNCHED ME OUT AN' TOOK OFF WITH THE CASH.
ANY IDEA WHY HE--?
ISN'T IT OBVIOUS? HE WAS DISGRUNTLED, MAN! NOT ONLY DID HE FEEL THAT I WAS MAKING HIM LOOK BAD, HE FELT YOU GUYS WEREN'T GIVIN' HIM THE RESPECT HE DESERVED!
Y'SEE, IN HIS MIND...
"...HE'S THE ONE WHO WAS BETRAYED."

AND YOU'RE SURE HE'LL HIT US AGAIN?
BUDDY, I GUARANTEE HE'LL HIT YOU AGAIN.
"WHEN?"
TAKE IT EASY ON THE SUDS, BIG FELLA...
"PROBABLY FIRST THING TOMORROW MORNING."
...WE'RE HITTIN' 'EM AGAIN, FIRST THING TOMORROW MORNING.

25
FREE 3-D
GLASSES
INCLUDED!
(SEE BACK COVER)

YEAH, SO... THE SITUATION IS THIS:
I'M LIKE, TOTALLY SCREWED.
DO TELL.
PREVIOUSLY
"DEADPOOL SOLD ME OUT! AND WORSE, HE LEFT ME HOLDING THE BAG! THE GUYS I'M WORKING FOR? THE CASINO OWNERS?
"THEY THINK I'M THE ONE THAT ROBBED THEM!"
THAT SLIMY, SCUMMY LITTLE...
WEASEL.
"AND WHY IS THAT?"
"BECAUSE THAT'S WHAT DEADPOOL TOLD 'EM!"
WHAT CAN I SAY? I THOUGHT HE WAS COOL, BUT...
...IT'S ALWAYS THE QUIET ONES, Y'KNOW?
"SURELY, HIS WORD ISN'T ENOUGH TO--"
"AND ALSO BECAUSE WE, LIKE, SWITCHED IDENTITIES! HE'S WEARING MY ARMOR..."
THE OL' SWITCHEROO!
...AND I'M WEARING HIS.
OH, DEAR. THAT WAS SIMPLY NOT A WISE DECISION ON YOUR PART.

WELL, YEAH... I KNOW THAT NOW, BUT--
CAN YOU NOT GO BACK TO YOUR EMPLOYERS AND EXPLAIN...?
THEY WON'T BELIEVE ME! WADE SET ME UP TO LOOK LIKE...I DUNNO, SOME KINDA--
--CLASSIC CASE OF A DISGRUNTLED EMPLOYEE WHO THOUGHT HE DESERVED MORE THAN WHAT HE WAS GETTING.
SO HE TOOK IT.
"HMM, YES. BLOODY REPREHENSIBLE. BUT REALLY, WEASEL...WHAT DID YOU EXPECT? IT'S DEADPOOL."
THAT'S HOW HE IS.
TRICKY
CONCLUSION

BLIND AL, I REALLY NEED HELP HERE...DO YOU HAVE ANY ADVICE FOR ME?
YES, RUN.
RUN AND DON'T LOOK BACK.
Y'MEAN GIVE UP? LET DEADPOOL WIN?!
WEASEL, MY DEAR, HE'S GOING TO WIN, ANYWAY--THAT'S THE WAY HIS GAME WORKS. THE MOMENT YOU PLAY YOU LOSE.
NO. UH-UH. THIS IS MY TOWN, AL...MINE. I'M ITS PROTECTOR.
EVEN THOUGH EVERYBODY'S HATIN' ON ME RIGHT NOW.
BUT THAT'LL CHANGE.
I'M TAKIN' WADE DOWN, AL--ONCE AND FOR ALL.
WEASEL, YOU'RE AN IDIOT.
NO.
I'M A HERO.

THIS IS MY MOMENT, AL...MY TIME TO SHINE. DEADPOOL'S OUT THERE PLOTTING SOMETHING, I KNOW IT. I'M GONNA MAKE SURE IT DOESN'T HAPPEN.
NOT IN MY CITY.
NOT ON MY WATCH!
B-BOOOOOOMMMMM!
AH, CRAP...

Y'KNOW HOW THEY SAY, "WHAT HAPPENS IN VEGAS, STAYS IN VEGAS"?
WELL, THIS JUST HAPPENED.
BOOM.
KOFF-KOFF! WHAT'S WITH ALL THE DAMN SMOKE?!
SORRY, PUSHED THE WRONG BUTTON.
WELL, TURN IT OFF!
YEEAH...KINDA DON'T KNOW HOW TO DO THAT...

YEP, FIRST THING THIS MORNING.
THEY'RE HERE, SIR.
"JUST LIKE HE SAID."
NO WAY THEY EXPECTED US AGAIN THIS SOON. BUT THIS TIME, FORGET ABOUT THE COUNTING ROOM AND GO STRAIGHT FOR THE VAULT.
BUT THE VAULT'LL BE LOCKED, WON'T IT?
IT WILL BE IF YOU DON'T HURRY--GO! I'LL HANG BACK AND COVER OUR EXIT.
"WHEN'S DEADPOOL GONNA %#$#%$% SHOW UP?"
GOT A FEELING WE'LL BE HAVIN' COMPANY SOON...
"HE SAID HE'D BE HERE!"
"I JUST HOPE HE'S WEARING HIS ARMOR, SIR--IF PEOPLE WERE TO FIND OUT THAT DEADPOOL IS WILDCARD..."
"WHEN I TALKED TO HIM LAST NIGHT, HE PROMISED THAT HE WOULD BE..."
TIME TO PAY, YOU TRAITOROUS BASTARD...
"YOU DON'T THINK HE'D SCREW US, DO YOU?"

I WOULDN'T BET AGAINST IT.
WHAT THE HELL'S *HAPPENING* DOWN THERE?! I CAN'T SEE ANYTHING 'CAUSE OF ALL THE DAMN *SMOKE!*
SECURITY SAYS THE GAMING FLOOR HAS BEEN SAFELY EVACUATED, SIR.
SIR!
"GRIZZLY'S ALMOST TO THE VAULT!"
%&#$... WILL IT HOLD?
THE ENGINEERS SAY "YES", BUT...
DAMMIT, *WHERE THE &#%$ IS HE?!*
SIR?
THERE YOU ARE!
"DEADPOOL--I MEAN WILDCARD HAS ENTERED THE BUILDING."
KRAAANNGG!

YOU UNBELIEVABLE DIRTBAG!
I ALWAYS KNEW YOU WERE SLIMY, BUT THIS?
CHOOOM! CHOOOM! CHOOOM!
BETRAYING ME LIKE THIS?!
KLAK-KLAK-KLAK-KLAK-KLIK-!
WE USED TO BE FRIENDS, MAN.

DUDE.
KLAK-KLAK-KLAK-KLAK-KLIK-!
YOU GOTTA STOP LIVIN' IN THE PAST.

"I MEAN, LOOK AROUND YOU!
"THIS IS A WORLD OF OPPORTUNITY! EVERYTHING'S FOR THE TAKING!
"ALL YOU HAVE TO DO IS REACH OUT...
"...AND GRAB IT."
YOU HAVE ONLY BEGUN TO DISCOVER YOUR POWER. JOIN ME...AND I WILL COMPLETE YOUR TRAINING.
WITH OUR COMBINED STRENGTH, WE CAN END THIS DESTRUCTIVE CONFLICT AND BRING ORDER TO LAS VEGAS.
K-CHOOOOOOMMM!
I'LL NEVER JOIN YOU!

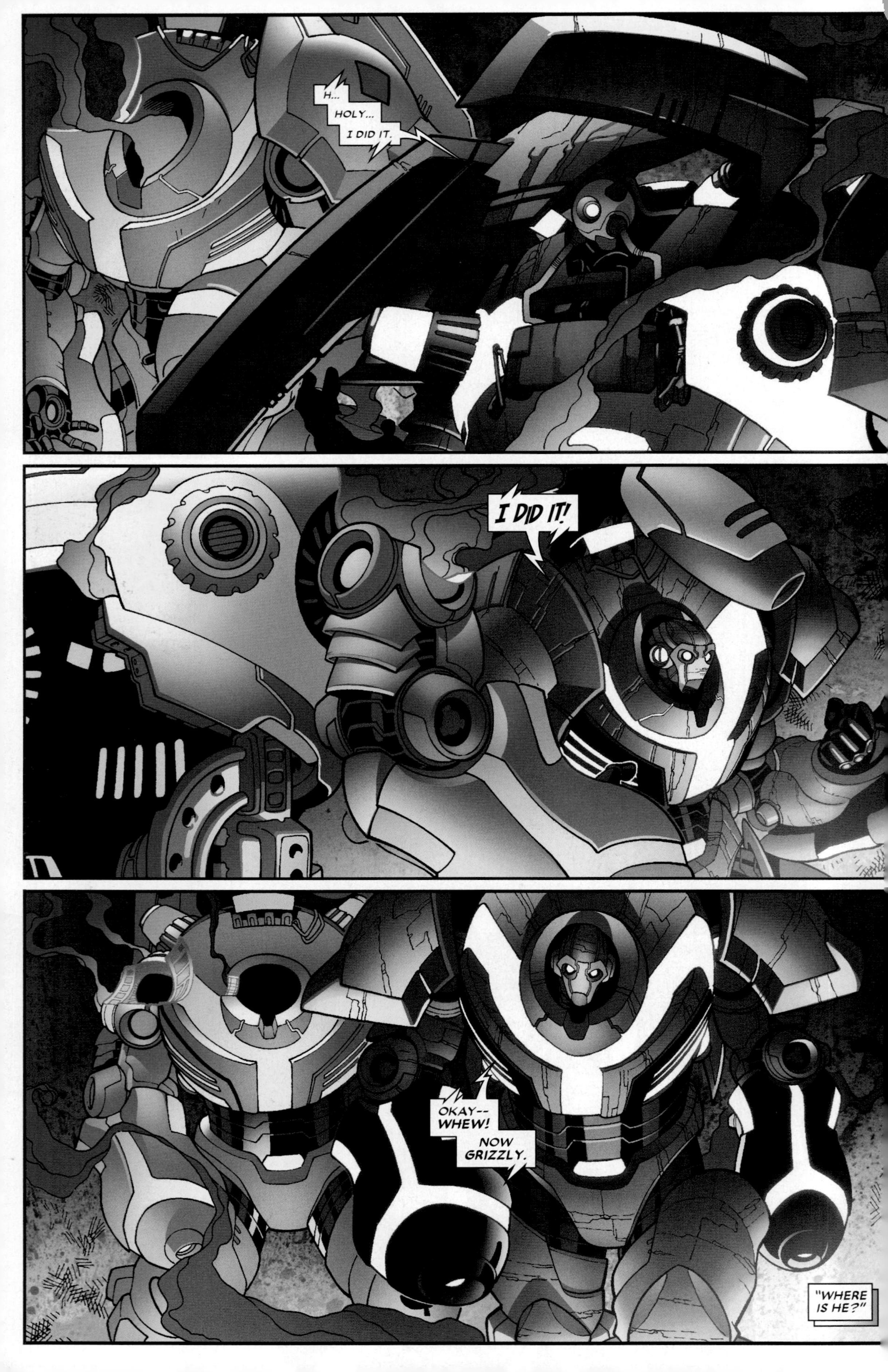
H...
HOLY...
I DID IT.
I DID IT!
OKAY--
WHEW!
NOW
GRIZZLY.
"WHERE IS HE?"

IN THE VAULT.
COOL.
"LOCK 'IM UP."
WHAT THE--?
K-KLANGGG!
BOOOOOMMM!
NOO!
SON OF A...

GOOD JOB ALL AROUND, "WILDCARD."
LET'S MAKE THIS QUICK--I'M LOSIN' MONEY.
GO OUT AND TAKE A BOW WHILE WE GET A CLEAN-UP CREW IN HERE.
UHH...
...O-OKAY?
WHERE'S--?
GRIZZLY? SOME HEAVIES FROM THE RAFT PRISON ARE ON THEIR WAY TO PICK HIM UP. SEEMS THEY'R EVEN MORE INTERESTED IN TUCKING HIM AWAY QUIETLY THAN WE ARE, HIM BEING AN ESCAPEE...
YOU ALL RIGHT? YOU SEEM A BIT... SHAKEN UP.
UH, YEAH! I MEAN...I'M FINE!
LOOK, I KNOW YOU TWO HAD HISTORY, BUT YOU MADE THE RIGHT DECISION.
YOUR "FRIEND" WEASEL? WAS A LOW-LIFE, BACK-STABBING DIRTBAG.
WELL, THAT SEEMS KINDA... HARSH...
IT'S THE TRUTH. AND YOU KNOW WHAT, DEADPOOL?
"HE GOT WHAT HE DESERVED."
YEEEAAAAAHH

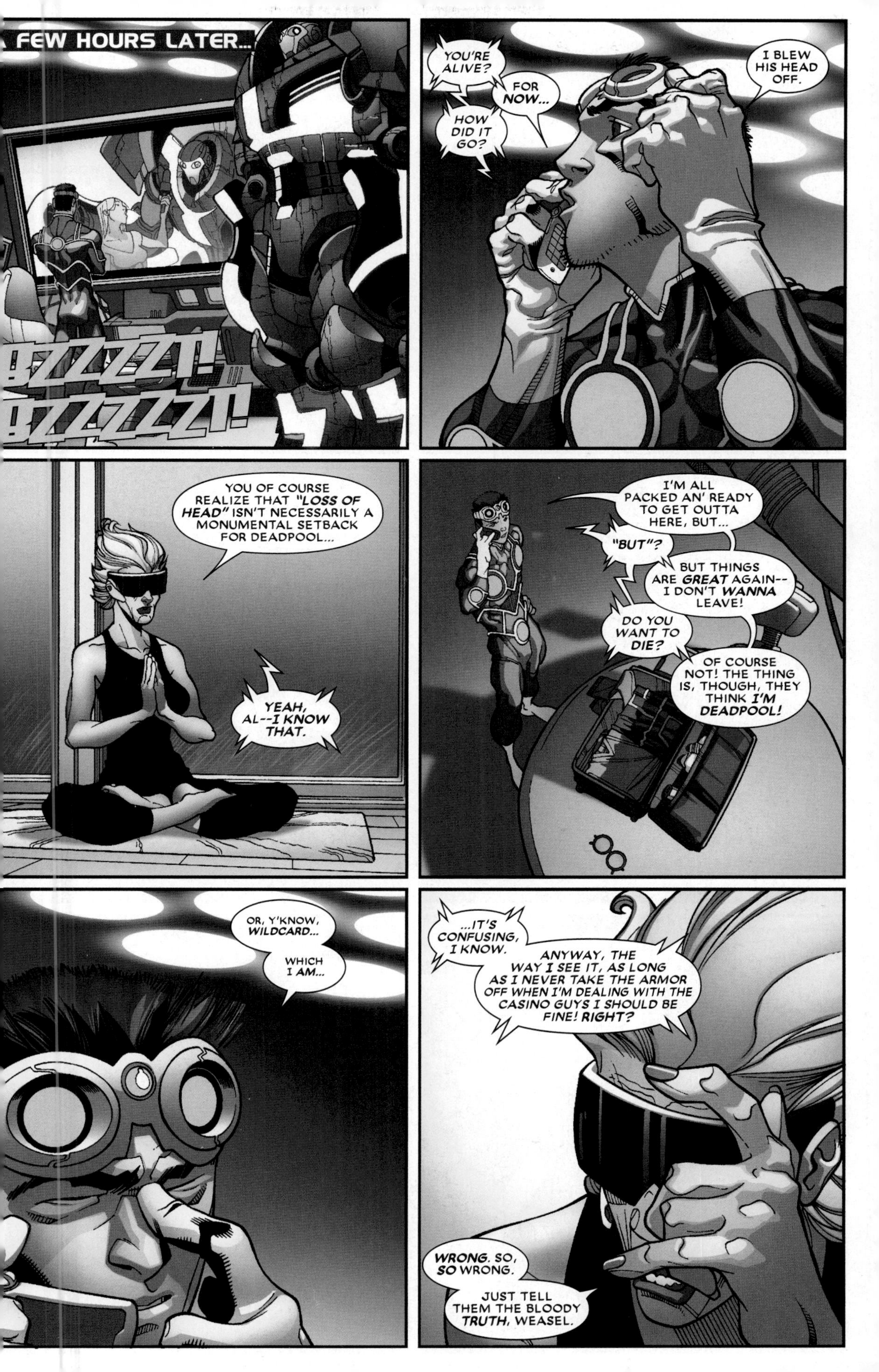
FEW HOURS LATER...
BZZZZZT!
BZZZZZT!
YOU'RE ALIVE?
FOR NOW...
HOW DID IT GO?
I BLEW HIS HEAD OFF.
YOU OF COURSE REALIZE THAT "LOSS OF HEAD" ISN'T NECESSARILY A MONUMENTAL SETBACK FOR DEADPOOL...
YEAH, AL--I KNOW THAT.
I'M ALL PACKED AN' READY TO GET OUTTA HERE, BUT...
"BUT"?
BUT THINGS ARE GREAT AGAIN-- I DON'T WANNA LEAVE!
DO YOU WANT TO DIE?
OF COURSE NOT! THE THING IS, THOUGH, THEY THINK I'M DEADPOOL!
OR, Y'KNOW, WILDCARD...
WHICH I AM...
...IT'S CONFUSING, I KNOW.
ANYWAY, THE WAY I SEE IT, AS LONG AS I NEVER TAKE THE ARMOR OFF WHEN I'M DEALING WITH THE CASINO GUYS I SHOULD BE FINE! RIGHT?
WRONG. SO, SO WRONG.
JUST TELL THEM THE BLOODY TRUTH, WEASEL.

BUT...WHO WOULD BELIEVE THE TRUTH?
THEY WILL-- YOUR CASINO FRIENDS.
WHEN THEY FIND DEADPOOL'S BODY.
IF MEMORY SERVES, IT TAKES HIM QUITE A WHILE TO RE-GROW A HEAD...
HOLY...YOU'RE RIGHT! WHEN THEY FIND HIS BODY, THEY'LL KNOW I'M NOT HIM! OR, Y'KNOW, HE'S NOT ME!
NOT WILDCARD, I MEAN!
I'M GONNA CALL 'EM RIGHT--
BZZZT--
--HEY, HOW 'BOUT THAT? THEY'RE CALLING ME!
THANKS, AL! I'M SAVED!
HELLO?
WE HAVE A PROBLEM. THE CLEAN-UP CREW WAS CRATING UP THE HOUSE'S ARMOR TO SEND TO THE LANDFILL WHEN THEY MADE A...TROUBLING DISCOVERY.
WOULD YOU CARE TO GUESS WHAT IT WAS?
ACTUALLY, I KNOW WHAT IT WAS.
AND I CAN EXPLAIN.
REALLY, DEADPOOL?

YOU CAN EXPLAIN HOW WEASEL'S BODY JUST... VANISHED?
WELL?
I'M WAITING...

BAD NEWS, I TAKE IT?
AAAK--!
H-HOW'D YOU--?
SNEAK OUT?
YEAH!
EASY.
EARLIER:
"I JUST, YOU KNOW...
YOU HAVE ONLY BEGUN TO UNDERSTAND YOUR POWER. JOIN ME.
"...SNUCK OUT."

BUT... WHY DIDN'T I--?
SEE ME?
EVEN EARLIER
KOFF-KOFF! WHAT'S WITH ALL THE DAMN SMOKE?!
OMETIME IN BETWEEN
"...AND GRIZZLY?"
"SCREWED HIM OVER."
JUST LIKE YOU DID ME.
YEP!
I'D SAY THAT ABOUT SUMS IT UP, WOULDN'T YOU?
YEAH. I GUESS IT DOES.
SO NOW YOU'RE GONNA KILL ME, RIGHT?
WHAT?!
OF COURSE NOT!

I'M A HERO, DUDE--HEROES DON'T GO AROUND KILLING PEOPLE, WILLY-NILLY!
SO...NOW YOU'RE GONNA KILL ME?
OH, FOR...
I'M NOT GONNA KILL YOU! IS THAT CLEAR? AS A MATTER OF FACT, I'M GONNA HELP YOU OUTTA THIS JAM!
THAT YOU CREATED.
YOU'RE NOT SEEING THE BIG PICTURE HERE.
YOU WERE A CRAPPY HERO, DUDE. LET'S FACE IT--SOONER OR LATER, YOU WERE GONNA BLOW IT.
BUT NOW, WITH ME TAKING OVER--
WAIT, YOU'RE TAKING OVER? TAKING OVER WHAT?
THAT.
DUH.
BUT... WHAT ABOUT ME?
YOU'RE GONNA HAFTA DISAPPEAR.

I KNEW IT--!
WEASEL.
FOR THE LAST TIME, I'M NOT GONNA KILL YOU. BUT YOU ARE GONNA HAFTA GO SOMEWHERE TO LAY LOW...FOR YOUR OWN PROTECTION.
YOU ARE, AFTER ALL, A WANTED FUGITIVE.
GREAT. THANKS.
WHERE AM I GONNA GO?
I THINK WE BOTH KNOW THE ANSWER TO THAT ONE, BUDDY...

THE NEXT DAY:
WILDCARD.
SO GLAD YOU COULD MAKE IT...AN HOUR LATE.
JUSTICE MAY NEVER SLEEP, BUT I DO--ESPECIALLY ON WEDNESDAYS.
IT'S FRIDAY.
AND FRIDAYS. YOU DIDN'T LET ME FINISH.
SO...YOU SAID YOU'VE TAKEN CARE OF WEASEL?
SURE DID...
CARE TO TELL US HOW?
I PUT HIM IN A BOX.
OKAY! GOOD MEETING, FELLAS--REALLY GOOD STUFF WE DID SOME REALLY IMPORTANT THINGS TODAY.
SEE YOU IN... TWO WEEKS? THREE?
SIT.
OOOO-KAY...?
YOU DON'T QUITE SEEM TO UNDERSTAND SOMETHING--YOU WORK FOR US NOW.
AS CHIEF OF SECURITY, WE EXPECT YOU TO BRIEF US EVERY MORNING AND EVERY NIGHT ON ANY CURRENT OR EMERGING THREATS TO OUR ENTERPRISE.
GEEZ, YOU MAKE IT SOUND LIKE A JOB...
IT IS A JOB.

I...
...HAVE A JOB?!
NNNNOOOOOOOOOO!

26
BANG!
JOHNSON

MOJAVE DESERT, 65 MILES NORTHWEST OF LAS VEGAS
CAFE
MORE COFFEE?
NAH, I'M GOOD.
THIS COVER IT?
UHH... YEAH, THAT'S MORE THAN--
JUST KEEP IT.
WHEW!
THAT YOUR BIKE OUT FRONT?
YEAH.
WELL, BE CAREFUL--IT'S ALREADY OVER A HUNDRED DEGREES OUT THERE, AN' THE WEATHER MAN SAYS IT'S JUST GONNA GET HOTTER.
THE WEATHER MAN'S RIGHT.

SINNER-SINNER, CHICKEN DINNER

AS VEGAS
WHATTA YA MEAN, "I QUIT"?
I MEAN, UH...
...I QUIT?
THIS JOB SUCKS AN' I DON'T WANNA DO IT ANY MORE?
WE HAVE AN AGREEMENT! *
GOOD POINT.
HOWEVER, I HAVE...
* SEE LAST ISSUE.
...A GUN.
HAVE I MADE MY POSITION CLEAR?
THOUGHT SO.

GO AHEAD. LEAVE.
AWESOME! SEE YA NEVER!
WE CAN GET ANY IDIOT TO WEAR THAT SUIT-- THERE WAS NEVER ANYTHING SPECIAL ABOUT YOU.
NOW, SEE... YOU REALLY SHOULDN'T HAVE SAID THAT.
AAAIIIEEEE!
BASH!
CRASH!
NO! PLEASE STOP--
AAAAGGH!!
AH, MUCH BETTER.
That was not very heroic of us.
OH, BUT I DISAGREE!
THOSE GUYS ARE EVIL, MAN-- THEY PREY ON PEOPLE'S WEAKNESSES! HOW MANY PEOPLE'S LIVES HAVE THEY RUINED? AND FOR WHAT?
MONEY. THAT'S WHAT.
AND ARE YOU JUST GONNA STAND THERE LOOKIN' SCARY? OR ARE YOU ACTUALLY GONNA SAY SOMETHING?

WHY SHOULD I?
YOU'VE SAID IT ALL.
GHKK--!
CH-CHANK!
HOLD ON TIGHT, WADE.
I'M TAKIN' YOU FOR A RIDE.
KAARRRRR-RRRRRROOOOOOOMMMMMM!

IT'S BEEN A LONG TIME COMING, BUT YOU WILL NOW FACE VENGEANCE.
YOU WILL PAY FOR YOUR TRANSGRESSIONS.
MY WHAT?!
LOOK IF THIS IS ABOUT THOSE UNPAID PARKING TICKETS, I CAN--!
YOU'RE AN ASSASSIN!
DRIVE
CAREFULLY
Come Back
SOON
I'M NOT AN ASSASSIN, I'M A--AAOW!--MERCENARY!
THERE'S A DIFFERENCE!
NOT TO ME.

WELL, I GUESS I COULD EXPLAIN THE MANY AND VARIED DIFFERENCES BETWEEN THE TWO...
OR...
WHOOOSH!
...I COULD JUST DO THIS.
KKKKKRRRRRRRRRRRRRRR--!

BLAM!
BLAM!
BLAM!
BLAM!
BLAM!
BLAM!
KRRA-AAAROOOOOOMMMM

OOO-
OOOH...
YEP, THAT'S BROKEN.
And so's that.
YEAH...
LOOKIN' BACK, THAT PROBABLY WASN'T...THE BEST IDEA...
WWHROOOSHHH!
YOU'RE GODDAMN RIGHT IT WASN'T.
OH, FOR...
HGGK--!

LOOK INTO MY EYES, *WADE WILSON...*
...AND FEEL THE PAIN OF PENANCE *LONG OVERDUE.*
WHAT... THE #$%& ARE YOU TALKIN' ABOUT?!
MY PENANCE STARE WILL REVE
ALL OF YOUR PAST SINS TO YO
YOU WILL SEE THROUGH TH
EYES OF THOSE YOU HAVE
WRONGED, THOSE YOU HAVE
DESTROYED.
HEH... SO, LIKE A *HIGHLIGHT* REEL?
YES.
WELL, WHAT'RE YOU *WAITIN'* FOR?
ROLL THE #$&%#& TAPE.

FFWA
HHHHHH!
WHAT THE HELL...?

HUKK--!
KK--!
HOLD ON... YOU'VE GOT A TUBE DOWN YOUR THROAT.
ALMOST...
...THERE.
AGHK--!
KOFF! KOFF!
WHY... AM I HERE?
BECAUSE YOU SURVIVED.
WITH A LITTLE HELP.
DO YOU REMEMBER HANGING YOURSELF?

DO YOU REMEMBER WHY?
YEAH.
LIFE WAS-- KOFF!--#$%&, ANYWAY. BETTER TO JUST...GET IT OVER WITH.
YOU'RE NINETEEN.
EIGHTEEN.
NINETEEN.
YOU'VE BEEN IN A COMA FOR TWENTY-ONE DAYS. YOUR BIRTHDAY WAS TWO DAYS AGO.
YOUR FUNERAL WAS NINE DAYS AGO.
DON'T FEEL BAD THAT YOU MISSED IT--NOBODY ELSE SHOWED UP, EITHER.
YOU DON'T HAVE MANY FRIENDS, DO YOU, WADE?

OSCAR ZERO IS A CLANDESTINE, SELF-SUFFICIENT CELL OF AGENTS OPERATING UNDER THE GUIDANCE OF THE CIA'S DIRECTORATE OF OPERATIONS, BUT OVERSEEN BY...WELL, NO ONE, REALLY.
IT'S NOT THAT THE SUITS DON'T WANNA KNOW WHAT WE DO, IT'S JUST THEY DON'T WANNA KNOW HOW WE DO IT.
WHAT DO YOU DO?
WE KILL PEOPLE.
WHAT KINDA PEOPLE?
THE KIND THAT DESERVE IT.
WE WANT YOU, WADE.
YOU HAVE MORE CLEAN KILLS THAN ANY THREE MEN IN YOUR BATTALION...AND YOU'VE NEVER EVEN SEEN COMBAT.

YEAH, WE KNOW. WE'VE BEEN WATCHING YOU FOR QUITE A WHILE.
WHAT IF I SAY NO?
YOU'LL GO BACK TO BEING DEAD...BUT THAT'S WHAT YOU WANTED, RIGHT? THE CHOICE IS ENTIRELY YOURS.
THIS IS YOUR SECOND CHANCE TO EITHER LIVE, OR DIE.

WHAT'S IT GONNA BE?

BRAKK-AKK-AKK-AKK-AKK-AKK-AKK

DAMN, WILSON...

...HOW 'BOUT SAVIN' SOME FOR THE *REST* OF US NEXT TIME?

WILSON?
H-WUKK!

ARE YOU *HIT?!*
NO, JUST FEEL...

SICK...

WELCOME BACK, WADE.
I'M... IN THE STATES?
OF COURSE! WHAT, YOU THOUGHT WE'D LEAVE YOU TO THE MERCY OF SOME THIRD WORLD MEDICINE MAN?
YOU'RE OUR TOP SCORER, MY MAN. ONLY THE BEST FOR YOU.
WHAT'S... WRONG WITH ME?
THAT'S A LOADED QUESTION...
ANSWER IT.
OKAY, YOU HAVE CANCER. LOTS OF CANCER. SOMETHING LIKE... THIRTY-ONE TUMORS?
THIRTY-FOUR.
THIRTY-FOUR.
CAN THEY CUT 'EM OUT?
NOPE, NOT WITHOUT KILLING YOU.
SO THAT'S IT. I'M DONE.
NOT NECESSARILY. WE'VE BEEN WORKING WITH CANADA ON A PROJECT THAT MAY BE ABLE TO HELP YOU, BUT IT'S VOLUNTEER-ONLY.
THE CHOICE IS ENTIRELY YOURS.
WHAT KINDA PROJECT?

HHH...
HHH...
HHH...
HRRRAAAAAAAAAAAAAHHHHHHH!

AAAAAAAHHHH!

YOU'RE HIM, RIGHT?
YOU'RE THE GHOST RIDER?
YEAH.
SOMETIMES.
WELL, I'M DEADPOOL.
ALL THE TIME.
AN' I DON'T NEED TO BE REMINDED OF IT.
WHAT DID YOU SEE?

NOTHIN' I HAVEN'T SEEN BEFORE.
WHICH WAY TO TOWN?
THAT WAY.
'BOUT EIGHTY MILES.
%#!&.
CAN YOU, LIKE, FIX THAT THING? WITH YOUR GHOST POWERS?
NO.
BUT I CAN FIX IT WITH THESE.

ALL DONE.
LET'S RIDE.
SOMEBODY ONCE TOLD ME THAT, AT THE END OF IT ALL, WHAT WE REGRET ISN'T WHAT WE'VE DONE, BUT WHAT WE DIDN'T DO.
YEAH, THAT SOUNDS ABOUT RIGHT.
DID YOU COME AFTER ME TO KILL ME?
I DIDN'T COME AFTER YOU. IT DID. THE GHOST RIDER.
AN' NO.
I THINK IT WANTED YOU TO SEE SOMETHIN'. IF IT'D MEANT TO KILL YOU, YOU'D BE DEAD.
DO YOU THINK I... DESERVE TO DIE?
BASED ON WHAT I KNOW ABOUT YOU?
YEAH.

THANKS, MAN.
END

BONUS STORY!!!
LOOK AT THESE GEEKS.
RAIDING THIS OFFICE FOR CORPORATE SECRETS, FUMBLING AROUND WITH THAT STEEL-REINFORCED SAFE.
DON'T THEY KNOW YOU NEED, LIKE, A THERMAL LANCE TO GET THROUGH SOMETHING AS THICK AS THAT?
Thermal lance, check.
FUHWOOOOSHHHHHH
FORTUNATELY, I CAN REGENERATE BODY PARTS--LIKE EYES.
UNFORTUNATELY, THAT TAKES SOME TIME.
How long?
'BOUT TEN PAGES.

Unfortunately, they're all shooting at you now.
BURJ KHALIFA. TALLEST BUILDING IN THE WORLD.
And unfortunately, you've got about 124 stories until you kiss pavement.
DO YOU ALWAYS HAVE TO BE SUCH A DOWNER?

I CAN'T LET THESE JOKERS LEAVE THIS BUILDING ALIVE. OTHERWISE, I DON'T GET PAID.
KRESHHHH!
THESE CREEPS HAVE BEEN STEALING IDEAS FOR YEARS, AND I'VE BEEN HIRED TO DO SOMETHING ABOUT IT. SOMETHING PERMANENT.
OF COURSE BEING TEMPORARILY BLIND SUCKS.
SEE?
NOTHING COOL TO LOOK AT. YOU MIGHT AS WELL BE READING A FRIGGIN' BOOK.
LUCKY FOR YOU I'VE GOT POOL-O-VISION!
WITH POOL-O-VISION, I'M ABLE TAKE THE MOST MINUTE PIECES OF SENSORY DETAIL AND WEAVE THEM INTO AN ELABORATE FABRIC OF REALITY.
Wait a minute. There's no such thing as "Pool-O-Vision."
THIS WAY UP

THAT'S WHAT *YOU* THINK!
HELLO! CORPORATE BURGLARS! I'M COMIN' FOR YA!
What are you doing?
CLEVERLY DRAWING THEM OUT OF HIDING WITH THE SOUND OF MY VOICE.
Uh-huh.
HECK, I CAN PRACTICALLY ***HEAR*** BURGLAR #1 RIGHT AROUND THIS CORNER!
DAREDEVIL CAN SUCK IT.

HECK, I SHOULD DO ***ALL OF MY JOBS*** WITHOUT EYES...
Dude, seriously--
FREEZE, BAD GUY!

?!
DON'T MOVE A MUSCLE!

BA-BLAM
KONK
OKAY, SO MAYBE I WAS A LITTLE OFF...
Is your vision back yet? Because now they all know you're alive, and they'll be coming back to *finish you off.*
SCOUT ONE TO BASE...
DO ME A FAVOR AND TELL ME IF THIS IS A NEW SPOOL OF TAPE OR A REALLY OLD DONUT.
How the hell would I know? I'm just a voice inside your head.

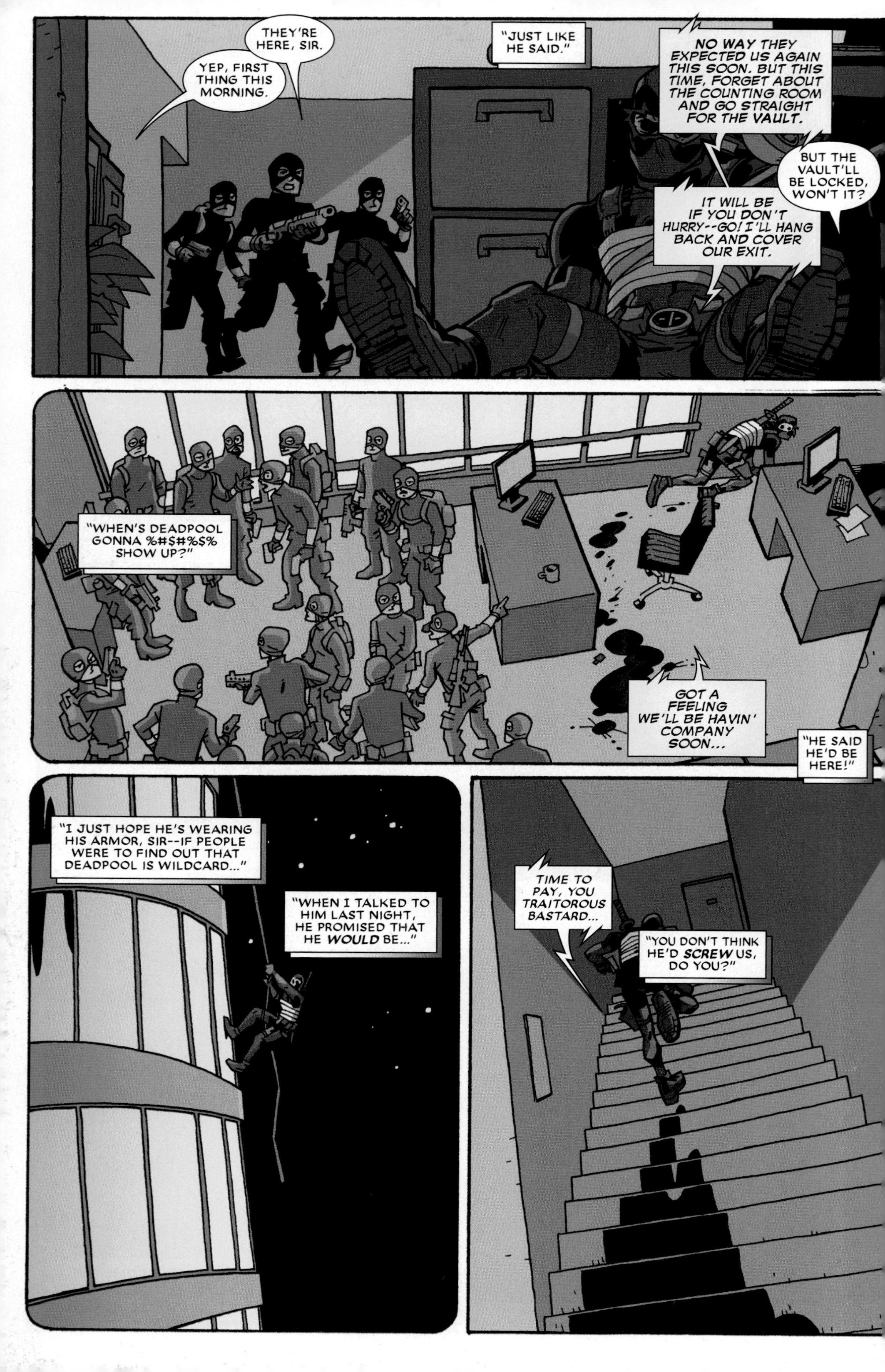
YEP, FIRST THING THIS MORNING.
THEY'RE HERE, SIR.
"JUST LIKE HE SAID."
NO WAY THEY EXPECTED US AGAIN THIS SOON. BUT THIS TIME, FORGET ABOUT THE COUNTING ROOM AND GO STRAIGHT FOR THE VAULT.
BUT THE VAULT'LL BE LOCKED, WON'T IT?
IT WILL BE IF YOU DON'T HURRY--GO! I'LL HANG BACK AND COVER OUR EXIT.
"WHEN'S DEADPOOL GONNA %#$#%$% SHOW UP?"
GOT A FEELING WE'LL BE HAVIN' COMPANY SOON...
"HE SAID HE'D BE HERE!"
"I JUST HOPE HE'S WEARING HIS ARMOR, SIR--IF PEOPLE WERE TO FIND OUT THAT DEADPOOL IS WILDCARD..."
"WHEN I TALKED TO HIM LAST NIGHT, HE PROMISED THAT HE WOULD BE..."
TIME TO PAY, YOU TRAITOROUS BASTARD...
"YOU DON'T THINK HE'D SCREW US, DO YOU?"

POP!
ZZ-ZZZ-ZZZZZZZZZT!
IF MY CALCULATIONS ARE CORRECT, THEN THIS WHOLE FLOOR IS NOW CAST IN UTTER AND COMPLETE DARKNESS.
YEAH, THAT'S RIGHT, CHUMPS. NOW LET'S SEE HOW YOU LIKE IT.
But...
SHHHH NOW.
I DON'T WANT YOU TIPPING THEM OFF.

RIGHT ABOUT NOW THEY SHOULD BE FUMBLING IN THE DARK, TERRIFIED OUT OF THEIR WEE LITTLE MINDS.
Let me know when it's over and you're dead.
DEAD? PLEASE. JUST WAITING FOR THE RIGHT MOMENT TO PUT THE--

--SHINE ON THEM!
‹ARGH! MY FRIGGIN' EYES!›
AAAARGH!
CAN'T SEE!!!
‹IT'S THE GOGGLES--THEY'RE INTENSIFYING THE FLARES! GET 'EM OFF, GET 'EM OFF!›
PLEASE. ALLOW ME.

HEY. WOW. MY VISION'S BACK!
Your timing, as usual, is impeccable.
YOU KNOW, I KIND OF PREFER THE POOL-O-VISION VERSION.
MAYBE I CAN FIND A SHARP STICK AROUND HERE SOMEWHERE...
LET IT SNOW, LET IT SNOW, LET IT SNOW...
END

FOLD HERE

SECTION 4, ARTICLE 8

FOLD THERE

MATERIALS NEEDED:

1) A blade (non-rusty), sword, scissors or comparable cutting utensil

2) Glue (if you have glue, skip to step 5)

3) An old or lame horse

4) A big blender

5) A steady hand (non-severed)

INSTRUCTIONS:

A)Cut the pieces out around the edges

B)Fold the flaps on the earpieces, match them accordingly & glue

C) Allow glue to dry or let your little brother wear glasses then laugh as they dry to his face and he has to get them surgically removed!

D) Put on glasses and see the wonders of our 3-D cover come to life as you experience it in...
High Definition 4-D!

*After purchase of book! (We're not running a charity here, folks!)

DEADPOOL #25 BACK COVER
Design by Nelson Ribeiro

DEADPOOL #25 COVER INKS
by Dexter Vines

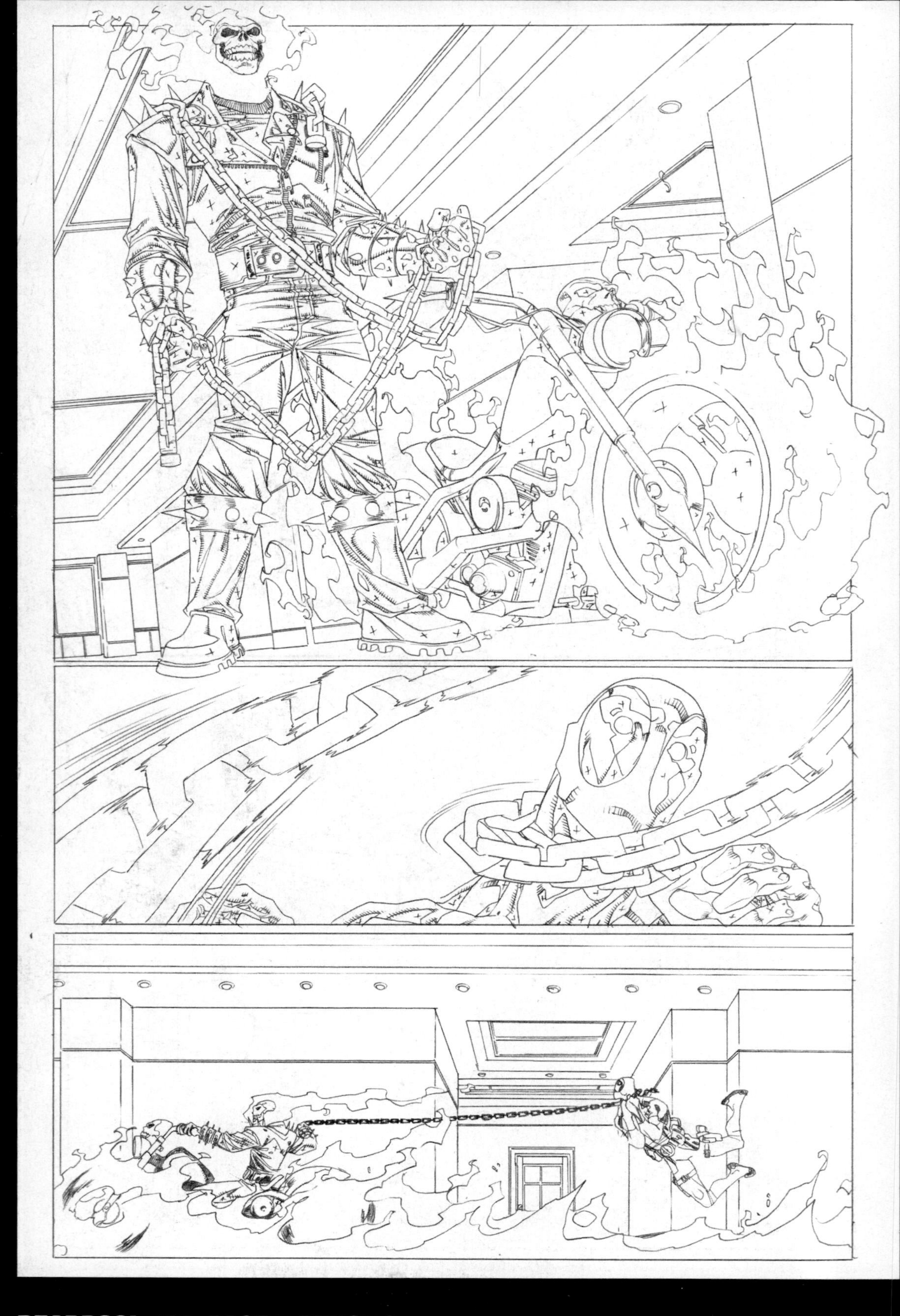

DEADPOOL #26, PAGE 5 PENCILS
by Carlo Barberi

DEADPOOL #26, PAGE 5 INKS
by Juan Vlasco

THE HOUSE